T

MESSENGER

By Arnie Harris

To Mike
with love
Arnie

Published by New Generation Publishing in 2019

First Edition

ISBN 978-1-78955-794-7

www.newgeneration-publishing.com

 New Generation Publishing

WRITER

I'd sit close to the window, to get some natural light
I'd turn on my computer, and hope that I could write
Maybe I'd make poetry, I'd done some – it's alright
Would I create a novel? I sometimes thought I might

I met a lot of authors, I looked at them in awe
I'd seen work that they'd produced, I wanted to read more
Could I ever write so well? I never had before
Would people want to read my work? I really wasn't sure

Could I find inspiration? Could I find each word?
If I was not succeeding, would I be undeterred?
Did I have enough talent? Was all this just absurd?
Maybe I just wouldn't try. Was backing out preferred?

Then I was encouraged, so believed that I could do it
I said "I am a writer" so everybody knew it
I'll write a book, decision made, I hope that I don't rue it
So when it's done please be kind, if you should review it

ABOUT THE AUTHOR

Arnie Harris was born in the East End of London to a British mother, and a father who had managed to leave Nazi occupied Austria in order to start a new life in England.

With a brother who is five years older, Arnie's love of sport and music followed a similar path to that of his much-loved sibling. In 1966, the year that the England football team became world champions at Wembley, the Harris family moved home to the same town when Arnie was eleven years old.

Although a grammar school student, Arnie could never claim to be academic and preferred to have a football at his feet rather than a textbook in his hands. Since retiring from full-time employment in 2016 after a successful career in sales and management positions, Arnie has been able to devote more time to writing and subsequently to producing **'The Messenger'**.

The author has one adult daughter, who lives just a short drive from the Hertfordshire home he shares with his partner.

Arnie's thoughts and views in the book, provide an insight into the man behind the words that may surprise even his closest friends.

This book is dedicated to my parents

Eva and Joe Harris

With love and gratitude xxx

'Never forgotten'

THE

MESSENGER

Contents

ABOUT THE BOOK

'**The Messenger**' is a collection of sincere, helpful messages which covers a variety of topics ranging from POSITIVITY, MOTIVATION and SELF-IMPROVEMENT to COMPASSION, FRIENDSHIP and CHARITY. The book includes important issues such as RACIAL HARMONY, BULLYING, STRESS and DEPRESSION, along with the author's thoughts on GROWING OLDER, PERSEVERANCE, GRATITUDE and many other subjects.

Presented in a unique style, the messages are easy to comprehend and can be used for encouragement and support, as well as for general advice on achieving a better and more contented life.

This enjoyable read is about matters that are part of everyday living for many of us, and seeks to show positive actions that could be put to use, in order to improve any given situation. Therefore, '**The Messenger**' can be an invaluable friend to the readers, at times of need or at important junctures in their lives.

GRATITUDE

Maybe I was dying
Of course I didn't know
My family were crying
Afraid that I might go

I was lying prostrate
Curtains round my bed
Don't know what was happening
Don't know what was said

Apparently I struggled
To claim another breath
Thankfully I found one
To save me from my death

The team worked hard around me
And fought for my existence
I couldn't battle much myself
For I had no resistance

Draining fluid from my lungs
They strove for my revival
Only one thing on their minds
Ensuring my survival

The reason I've composed the words
In all these written verses
Is to thank those people for my life
The doctors and the nurses

Thank you. Thank you very much.
xx

INTRODUCTION TO THE MESSENGER

When I suffered some health issues over the course of a number of years, there were some very difficult periods for me to deal with. These sometimes resulted in low mood and my rather negative outlook on life.

As I overcame each obstacle, I gradually started to feel better about myself, and my mind-set was changing considerably. Positivity and optimism for the future began to replace the previous negativity, and then after a horrific episode in hospital, my overriding emotion was of absolute gratitude for surviving the ordeal. This overwhelming gratitude I now had for life quickly expanded to other areas of my day-to-day world, and so I became incredibly thankful for everything I had, such as a loving family, good friends and a place called home.

In my new-found appreciation of life, I developed a better understanding of what happiness and love truly mean, of what encouragement and motivation can achieve and of how compassion and support really can heal. Before long, I felt the need to tell people about positive thinking, self-improvement, helping others and then various aspects of life and situations which could possibly become easier to manage, with just a change in thought or attitude. I soon realised that I had to write this book, so that people might benefit from what I have learned.

I genuinely feel that **'The Messenger'** will help the readers to cope with many different issues and to deal with life's problems. The book can bring them hope when life feels hopeless, it can give them motivation where it is lacking and it can be a great comfort when it is needed.

I think this book can show individuals how to live more contented lives, I believe it can teach them how to be more confident and I'm sure it will help them to improve as people. **'The Messenger'** can assist everyone who wants or needs to learn and grow, and maybe in a small way, it might contribute to the world becoming a better place.

The thought that I might inspire, motivate, encourage and generally help people, by putting these messages into such a simple format, has been a powerful driving force in pushing me to write the book.

I am immensely proud of **'The Messenger'**, and if it does have a positive influence on the readers, I will have achieved what I set out to do.

I hope you enjoy my book.

Love Arnie xx

THE
MESSENGER

THE RAGING FIRE

There's a raging fire within my soul
The flames are getting higher
You cannot keep me from my goal
You can't quell my desire

You can snigger in my face
Or talk behind my back
But I know I will reach that place
Now I am on this track

There's a growing urge within my heart
I know it can't be halted
Attempts to pull my plans apart
Be sure they will be thwarted

You can state "It can't be done"
And say that I won't make it
But I have the will, now I've begun
You really cannot break it

There's a power force within my brain

And it cannot be denied

There's no one who could halt my train

You will not stop my ride

Anything you want to say
I have already heard
So whatever game you try to play
I will not be deterred

I've an inner strength, and I know how

To use it as I need

There's nothing that can stop me now

I know I will succeed

ENOUGH

A bigger car, a pleasure cruise

A Gucci bag and Jimmy Choos

A private jet, a super yacht

One always wants more than they've got

A grander house or more than one

One for home, one in the sun

Swapping neighbours for a larger plot

One always wants more than they've got

Well I don't need all that stuff

All I ask for is enough

Enough to eat - don't need a lot

One always wants more than they've got

Enough real love, enough good health

Now that is my idea of wealth

I couldn't be happy, no matter what

If I always want more than I've got

PAY IT FORWARD

Caring will not hurt you

Compassion is a virtue

Don't let it desert you, pay it forward

When people show affection

And make a good connection

Follow their direction, pay it forward

If someone gives you time

And tries to help you climb

It wouldn't be a crime, to pay it forward

Being selfish is a blindness

So when we're offered kindness

We can use it to remind us, to pay it forward

If we would pay it forward

Be sure that many more would

Pay it forward, pay it forward, pay it forward

BROTHER

You might wear a scarf upon your head

Or a skull-cap might be what you choose

You might wear a gown from neck to toe

Or a prayer shawl in yellows and blues

Maybe you pray in a synagogue

In a temple or even at home

You might prefer to kneel in a church

Or a mosque that's the shape of a dome

We may have some different beliefs

We might have light or dark skin

To find where we have common ground

We may have to look within

Maybe you live in a certain way

Maybe I live in another

But I pray we can all live in peace

For you'll always be my brother

SCARED

If so many people hadn't been afraid

If so much real fear hadn't been displayed

When chances came if only they had dared

They might have won if they hadn't been so scared

They were doomed to fail because they were frightened

When they should've been brave their fear always
  heightened

With good opportunities, how might they have fared?

They might have succeeded if they hadn't been so scared

Now it is you who must overcome the fear

Your time for success could really be so near

Just make certain that you are well prepared

Then I'll be with you, so you needn't be so scared

RICH

Do you have a roof over your head?

A place you call home with a comfortable bed?

Do you keep yourself warm with central heating?

Is there food on the table, ready for eating?

Do you have family who love you and friends too, who care?

If you ever really need them do you know they'll be there?

Do you feel grateful that you are quite healthy?

Are you seeing it yet, the meaning of wealthy?

Now when you feel down and you think life's a bitch

Just look around you, you might just see you're rich

LAVENDER HILLS

Feeling so stressed

Scared and depressed

Concerns about paying the bills

Put them aside

Picture outside

And strolling in lavender hills

Needing to sleep

Counting the sheep

With thoughts about all of life's ills

Just close your eyes

Imagine blue skies

And strolling in lavender hills

Can't sort tonight

Turn out the light

Don't take any more of those pills

This day is done

Think of the sun

And strolling in lavender hills

THE BRIGHTER SIDE

If you're living in the dark

Where the shadows drench the souls

And the mortals only cart a heavy load

Where few can make their mark

And few will reach their goals

You are walking on the wrong side of the road

Come on over to the light

Where the positive way rules

And an optimistic view can't be denied

You'll be learning what is right

Though it isn't taught in schools

And you'll flourish with us on the brighter side

IF YOU NEVER

If you never risk a failure

You may never taste success

If you never push the boundaries

You may never quite progress

Step out from your comfort zone

I think that is essential

To make it much more likely

You'll reach your full potential

If you're so afraid to lose

That you don't try to win

Your hopes could come to an end

Before you would begin

So take a chance, make the call

You may be so surprised

To see the person you become

But hadn't recognised

LION

There are bridges I've crossed

There are mountains I've climbed

There are long roads that I've had to take

There are seas that I've swum

There are oceans I've sailed

There were times when my body would ache

There was pain I would suffer

There were scars I would carry

There were battles that I had to win

My heart it was burning

My faith I was losing

I thought I might really give in

I fought through the jungle

I needed to make it

And fight just as hard as I can

Against all I triumphed

Because I discovered

There's a lion inside this man

WISDOM

You will gain more knowledge

If you read page after page

But you'll become much wiser

Through experience and age

We learn from our mistakes

Don't be afraid to make them

So when chances come along

Make certain that you take them

Of course you should keep reading

And that's what I advise

But also learn from life itself

To be clever *and* be wise

SMILING EYES

You were the girl who skipped when you walked

You were the girl who sang when you talked

You were that girl, which no one denies

You were the girl with the smiling eyes

Now you're the lady who's choked up with tears

From all that's been hurting over the years

It's so sad to hear the pain in your cries

For I knew the girl with the smiling eyes

The way you are suffering is so hard to bear

The way you've been treated is just so unfair

The stream down your cheeks is no real surprise

But hold on to that girl with the smiling eyes

Let me tell you sweet lady that you are still strong

And you will be happy - it won't be too long

Once more you'll be shining like stars in the skies

You'll again be the girl with the smiling eyes

TOUGH LOVE

Maybe you can if you say you can
Be positive - it's the only way
You won't succeed if you have no plan
So put one into action today

Maybe you can if you would just try
Bring out some more of the optimist
Don't let the opportunities die
Grab chances now while they still exist

No one will come and knock on your door
To give you the help you are needing
There are no free lunches anymore
Those bleeding hearts can't keep on bleeding

It's time for you now to knuckle down
Just show the world what you can do
You have to swim so that you don't drown
Good fortune can then come to you

Don't think that I am not on your side
I am with you - don't ever forget
But if you're going to turn the tide
A big dose of tough love you will get

THE OLDER GENERATION

There is a group of people

Deserving of our respect

It is just the very least

These people should expect

Surely they have earned that right

They've done much for our nation

The group I am referring to

Is the older generation

'The older we get, the wiser we grow'

Is a theory I don't reject

So let's tap into their wisdom bank

For the pearls that we could collect

Give them help with what they need

Show them consideration

We should not ever forget

The older generation

BE THE REAL YOU

Don't try to conceal

How you really feel

Don't pretend if something's not good

Don't try to hide

What you are inside

Make certain that you're understood

Be the real you

In all that you do

To act out your life would just hurt you

So love who you are

Then you can go far

Don't let your true heart desert you

If you're not what folks need

Then you can be freed

To be just who you want to be

Rather than shrinking

Say what you're thinking

And stand up and shout "I am me"

A BETTER PLACE

The world would be a better place

If everyone could try to see

That anywhere we choose to live

We can in perfect harmony

The world would be a better place

If people could appreciate

That we may have our different faiths

But that's no reason we should hate

The world would be a better place

If all the bloody wars would cease

If we'd realise we're all the same

We could forever live in peace

SNAKES AND LADDERS

There are many ladders you can climb

There are also many snakes

There are times that you may reach the heights

And times you'll make mistakes

Occasions when you can roll the dice

Can crop up when you least expect it

So when a chance does come your way

Be certain that you won't reject it

It's true to say, in any game

That you can't always win it

But you will never taste victory

Unless you choose to be in it

So enter for the game of life

Where you'll climb and you may slide

For at least then you'll be proud to say

'At every chance I tried'

FOR LOVE

My eyes were burned through salty tears

My heart was filled with aching pain

But I know for sure, despite the fears

I'd risk it all for love again

FALL

You're feeling very low

You want to stay in bed

Those dark and heavy clouds

Cause pressure in your head

You just don't want to think

You don't want to get dressed

You're struggling just to move

You're feeling so depressed

Some people bring you down

With what they say to you

Including so called friends

You wish you never knew

I think of how you were

When you stood proud and tall

And now I'm here to help you

You'll recover from the fall

A MILE IN MY SHOES

It is easy for you to say that I was wrong

It is all very well to criticise

Easy to say that I was weak - though I was strong

When you can't see any tears in my eyes

You think I was bad and you shout that I'm a fool

You don't see the things I had to choose

You can't say what I've done is really very cruel

Until you've walked a mile in my shoes

You pour scorn on my reasons - mocking all the while

You laugh when you hear my decision

You look down on me with that condescending smile

You treat me with constant derision

You come to your conclusions - hearing from one side

Though you know there will be other views

So don't give your opinion and spread your gossip wide

Until you've walked a mile in my shoes

ENVY

Why would you be envious
Of what somebody owns?
Put away those feelings
Silence all your moans

Why on Earth should you care
What someone else has got?
It's none of your business
You shouldn't give a jot

Why aren't you happy
When a friend is doing well?
If you were a good friend
You'd be pleased as Hell

It's likely you have many things
That they might want or need
So don't wish for more and more
It is verging on pure greed

Now understand what matters

Is not expensive things

Necklaces and bracelets

Or shiny diamond rings

If there's love all around you

And your mind and body's healthy

You may have so much more

Than people who are wealthy

So when you look at others

You never should compare

For you might be seeing happiness

That isn't even there

Go count all your blessings

Instead of money in the banks

Cut out all that envy

And for all you have... give thanks

GOAL

What are you capable of?

What could you achieve?

There are few limitations

If you just believe

Realise that you are unique

And you have the skill

You can get to where you want

If you have the will

If you add determination

Give your heart and soul

There's a good chance you will make it

You can reach your goal

MILLIONS

Millions are dying in faraway lands

Millions are crying with head in their hands

Millions are needing clean water to drink

Millions are starving – their lives on the brink

Millions are raised to combat starvation

Millions are used to buy medication

Millions that we will continue to send

For millions who hope their darkness will end

But why just send money? Let's send engineers

Install irrigation that will serve them for years

Lay down the pipelines for constant clean water

Think of lives saved and lives it would alter

Send out the farmers who could then show them

When to sow seeds and how they should grow them

Those faraway lands may still need millions more

But millions would live longer than ever before

SPREAD THE LOVE

My spring and summer are over

So now that I've reached the fall

I hope I've gained enough wisdom

To give some advice to you all

The main thing I've learned for certain

Is that love is what life's all about

Believe that without love there's nothing

Of that I don't have any doubt

So pass on the word to all people

And spread it like never before

Then when you think you've done it enough

Go spread all the love a bit more

THEN AND NOW

You've made some mistakes
Well, haven't we all?
There are times when we climb
And times when we fall

You made some wrong calls
When you had better choices
You took some advice
But you heard the wrong voices

You think that you've failed
You forget your successes
You remember the noes
But none of the yeses

You have little confidence
And low self-esteem
You may have lost sight
Of what was your dream

So now I will tell you

How great you are

You've done so much good

And you've come so far

Just start believing

You're smart and you're wise

And know that's the truth

It's there in your eyes

I will encourage

And motivate you

Now look in the mirror

You'll see things anew

There's your reflection

What do you see?

The face of a person

Who used to be me

FRIEND

We know at times life can be hard

The problems don't seem to end

But others have their problems too

So remember to be a friend

We can get wrapped up in our woes

And although it's not what we intend

We forget some people might need us

So remember to be a friend

They'll listen to all your complaints

But an ear you must also lend

It cannot be just about you

So remember to be a friend

Friendships have to work both ways

So here's what I recommend

Be there for them as you should

And remember to be a friend

POSITIVE MIND

I know that you're thinking
It's easy for me to say
But I just want to help you
To live a better way

I want you to be positive
With an optimistic view
I'm trying now to teach you that
And explain what you should do

I was often negative
But I've changed my thinking now
Give me just a little time
So I can show you how

You could then look back and say
"I learned and then I grew"
I'd love to see you reach new heights
Heights you never knew

If you want to win in life
You must first win in your mind
Then success can come your way
And happiness you'll find

And when you reach a better place
I'll be glad and so proud too
That you believed and you achieved
By being a positive you

ANGER

You say someone enraged you

Though I'm not sure that's the case

For only your reaction

Took the smile right off your face

No one can make you angry

That is just your choice

You can choose to ignore them

Their voice is just their voice

If they try to provoke you

You could turn the other cheek

There's no need to respond

There's no need for you to speak

Don't get angry - walk away

Or else the mood could worsen

Do not let your temper rise

Just be the bigger person

THE ROLE MODEL

The muscled man walked down the street
A boxer he had been
He saw a boy with knife in hand
Was this a gangland scene?

Another boy lay at the feet
Of that boy with the knife
And while two gangs just stood and bayed
He feared for his young life

The muscled man then took a chance
And walked towards the boys
"Please stop and think" He said aloud
Then silence broke the noise

"I was once where you are now
I chose a life of crime
Dealing drugs and using blades
Soon I was doing time"

"I learned to fight inside the ring
It gave me self-respect
I tell you that what happened next
Is not what you'd expect"

"Boys like you looked up to me
That was a great surprise
If you would like a better life
Here's what I advise"

"Come with me down to the club
There is a gym inside
Let out some aggression there
And also gain some pride"

The boy with knife looked behind
To see his friends' blank faces
Then turned to face the muscled man
And walked ahead three paces

There was tension in the air
The boy remained so calm
He raised the knife towards the man...
And placed it in his palm

The boy looked down at the one
Still laying in the street
He then offered out his hand
And pulled him to his feet

Two gangs as one took the walk
Down to the local gym
They'd found a great role model
They're forever thanking him

STORM

It's true we all have testing times

Much harder days than the norm

So force a smile through gritted teeth

And you will weather the storm

You can emerge on the other side

To feel there wasn't much harm

Try to remember all things will pass

And after a storm there is calm

Whatever may hurt, whatever is wrong

You can turn it around or remove

All the pain in your mind or in your heart

Believe it will surely improve

But if there's a time you can't fight it alone

Be certain we'll fight it together

Then when it's all over you will realise

It was just one more storm you could weather

SKIN

Black, brown or white skin matters not

So let these words be spread

Think only of what's in our hearts

The blood is always red

DON'T GIVE UP

You should strain every sinew

And give all that's within you

Just make sure you continue

Don't give up

Yes, you may have been crying

But your eyes will be drying

So be sure to keep trying

Don't give up

Some people wish to block you

And others want to mock you

You cannot let them knock you

Don't give up

No you cannot be deterred

By some things you overheard

Perseverance is the word

Don't give up

BULLY

You can scream and you can shout
You can spit your venom out
Call me all the names you can call

You can rage and you can curse
You might threaten something worse
It will not affect me at all

You may spread all of your lies
Hide behind those hateful eyes
Try to inflict pain out of spite

Though you'd side with the devil
I won't sink to your level
I'll do what I think to be right

Your language is distasteful
Behaviour quite disgraceful
Thinking you're the big fish in town

Whatever you are saying
The actions you're displaying
Never ever will bring me down

WHY

Why is your sun never shining?

Why is your sky never blue?

Why are your birds never singing?

Why are your dawns never new?

Why is your heart never leaping?

Why do your lips never smile?

Why are your eyes never laughing?

Why are you sad all the while?

Why is your world never loving?

Why is your day never light?

Why is your mood never lifting?

Why is your life never bright?

If only you'd give me some answers

Then maybe we could turn the tide

I'd always be ready to help you

I'd always be right by your side

LIVE YOUR LIFE

To golden sands and seas of blue

With cloudless skies enjoy the view

Go to places you can reach

In foreign lands with native speech

Explore the sights and eat good food

Laze in the sun to lift your mood

Or take a drive with special friends

Catch the moments through the lens

See your children and laugh a lot

Appreciate the life you've got

But understand that time may fly

So try to live before you die

DREAMS

There was no war
Here's what I saw
Peace spread across all of the earth

No one was hated
Or alienated
That was my view for what it is worth

No starvation
In any nation
More than enough food and water

No young had died
No mothers cried
At the loss of a son or daughter

I so loved you
You loved me too
Yes that was how everything seemed

No more sorrow ...
Until tomorrow
For these were the dreams that I dreamed

STREETS OF LONDON

The pretty girl with golden hair
And just turned seventeen
Was walking roads of London Town
A place she'd never been

She'd left her home near Whitby Bay
With little time to pack
So everything she owned right now
She carried on her back

Her mother's man was doing wrong
Which her mum did not believe
So the pretty girl with golden hair
Felt she then had to leave

The girl then found a place to rest
And sat down for a minute
It was the doorway of a store
Just room for herself in it

A lady was then walking by
But felt compelled to stop
When she saw the teenage girl
Who shivered by the shop

The lady asked if they could talk
The girl then raised a smile
The lady crouched down by her side
They chatted for a while

The two walked off to a café
They sat down with a coke
She heard the girl's predicament
And then the lady spoke

"I'll find you a room for tonight
I'll pay for the hotel
One day you can pay me back
When you are doing well"

"Tomorrow, come to see me please
We'll see what we can do
If our meeting goes to plan
I'll have a job for you"

The girl asked "Why would a lady
Help someone she just meets?"
The lady said "I'll tell you
I once lived on the streets"

There are still thousands out there
And many cold nights braved
So it doesn't solve the problem
But at least this one was saved

TOMORROW

'Don't put off until tomorrow

What you can do today'

You've heard this many times before

And it's good to think that way

There are important things that you

Should really not delay

Realise there's a time for work

As well as time for play

Make that move, make a vow

That you won't hesitate

You have got to do it now

I hope that you don't wait

Now go ahead, no excuse

Don't procrastinate

For one of these tomorrows

Might just be too late

RISE

I wish you could manage

To open up your eyes

You might appreciate

The blue and sunny skies.

A new day has begun

So here's what I advise

Please try to get up now

I'll help to stop your cries.

For struggles that you face

I really sympathise

Try to battle through it

You can, please realise

You will not just give up

And all that it implies

Though you've sunk to the depths

Its time again to rise

THE OLDER MAN

There he goes, the older man

He walks with back so bent

His mind holds distant memories

Of carefree times once spent

The older man, he was once young

A very happy child

He'd often play out in the street

The man recalled and smiled

At eighteen years he went to war

So we could all be free

Many deaths and casualties

He wished he didn't see

He returned and found true love

Within a year he'd married

And though he'd had a peaceful life

The scars he always carried

Children came but grew and left

To live their lives elsewhere

Although they sometimes keep in touch

Their visits are so rare

He is now that older man

He's sad as he reflects

Because he is of no more use

He's a man no one respects

Give him a little of your time

Some kindness maybe due

Remember as the years go by

That you'll be older too

ONE STEP

When you might not have the courage

Or the confidence to start

When you foresee a bumpy ride

And unsure you have the heart

If you'd just make a small move

You could see your destination

That might be all that you need

To provide the motivation

So take it steady and get on course

And quite soon you will have begun

For a thousand miles a walk may be

But it starts with a step - just one

LEGACY

Ozone layer with expanding hole

Global warming from South to North Pole

Chopped down trees and many a plant

Bees need to live but sadly they can't

Animals of all kinds becoming extinct

The loss of God's creatures intrinsically linked

Oceans of plastic killing the fish

Is this a world for which we would wish?

Nations of evil killing for land

Or because of religions they don't understand

Hating and fighting due to colour of skin

These are the battles no one can win

Is this what we want for our children and theirs?

A world with no future where nobody cares?

Is this the legacy we'll leave behind?

Stop, or we could cause… the end of mankind

STARTING ALL OVER AGAIN

Things didn't go according to plan

So he brushed himself down and then

Set out to climb from a lowly rung

And started all over again

He fought through tough times for his return

He remembers it well, how and when

Determined he wouldn't stay down for long

He started all over again

And now that he's back and respected by all

He's considered a prince among men

But he'll never forget where he had once been

When he started all over again

TO HERE FROM ADVERSITY

Where did your voice go?

You had spoken loud in truth

Where was your backbone?

Had it weakened since your youth?

Where was your chest, sir?

That you'd puffed out in your shirt

Where had your heart gone?

Had you lost it through the hurt?

- - - - - - - - -

You've battled and returned, sir

Again we hear you clearly

You're standing tall and straight, sir

We're glad you're back sincerely

You're tougher now than ever

Your love is now so strong

We couldn't be more proud, now

You're back where you belong

THE ROAD

Just when you think your journey

Has slowed for the final bend

Something comes to refuel you

And life is your new-found friend

You're travelling along on a new road

There's nothing in the way

There's a light at the end of each tunnel

The forecast not so grey

So what has ignited the engine?

Is it a gift from above?

It's just what you always wanted

Days that are filled with love

HEART AND SOUL

Where does the courage come from?

Where does the battle start?

The answer to these questions

In my view is the heart

Without that drive to make things work

You're going nowhere fast

And though you might begin the ride

There's no way it can last

But what will help you find success

Achievement as a whole

Has to come from deep within

Which means giving all your soul

This could get you to where you want

And your effort would be true

As you'd be giving all you've got

That's the heart and soul of you

WISH YOU WERE HERE

I wish that you were here to see

What has now become of me

I'm positive in mind, it's clear

How I wish that you were here

I wish that you were here right now

To see that I have grown, and how

Confident with little fear

How I wish that you were here

I wish that you were here a while

To see me laugh, to see me smile

And no more shedding tear on tear

How I wish that you were here

I wish that you were here once more

To see I'm stronger than before

And happy with a love sincere

How I wish that you were here

I wish that you were here for good

I'd bring you home now if I could

I long to see you dancing near

How I wish that you were here

I wish that you were here, and then

I could say 'thank you' once again

For all you did for year on year

How I wish that you were here

I wish that you were here today

And for my lifetime you could stay

You're in my dreams but disappear

How I wish that you were here

I wish that you were here I swear

Or ... are you with me everywhere?

If that was true you'd hear me cheer

Oh how I wish that you were here

EXPECTATIONS

What do you expect of me?
To always do what's right?
That's not really possible
Though I try as I might

What do you expect of me?
To always say "That's good"?
That's not really feasible
Though I would if I could

What do you expect of me?
To always be right there?
I would not be capable
Though you know that I care

- - - - - -

What do you ask of yourself?
To run before you walk?
You are asking to trip up
If you choose to talk the talk

What do you ask of yourself?
To achieve the perfect score?
Hoping to win every battle
Fighting to win every war

Suffering with stress and sleepless nights
Could be some strong indications
That you should take some pressure off
With realistic expectations

LISTEN AND LEARN

You like the sound of your own voice

But you should try to hear

What others wish to say as well

Take notice, be sincere

You might like the attention

But sometimes you're too loud

There are others in the room

There are voices in the crowd

Talking less and listening more

Is a good learning technique

For you must already know

Of that you wish to speak

DON'T WASTE IT

If you have some talent
Or if you have a skill
Make sure you don't waste it
You've potential to fulfil

If you have some money
Some gold coins in the pot
Make sure you don't waste it
Be wise with what you've got

If you have some good health,
You are a lucky man
Make sure you don't waste it
Enjoy it while you can

If you have some real love
That's only meant for you
Make sure you don't waste it
And give some true love too

If you have a long life
With those so near and dear
Make sure you don't waste it
Be thankful that you're here

FLY

If your luck is down on the floor
When you think you can't take much more
As long as I know you will try
I'll be your wings so you can fly

If you're so sad that you can't smile
I'll lift your heart up by a mile
You won't need to ask how or why
I'll be your wings so you can fly

When you think that you just can't cope
If you feel like there is no hope
If you can't hear birds in the sky
I'll be your wings so you can fly

If you're struggling to carry on
And you're thinking all joy has gone
If you can't stem the tears you cry
I'll be your wings so you can fly

When you're feeling so very low
When you can't see the way to go
Don't drop your chin - hold your head high
I'll be your wings so you can fly

HELP

You should never be afraid to ask for help

You can't manage everything alone

You might be going through a difficult time

So you just have to pick up the phone

You could call a friend to ask for advice

Or just for a listening ear

It could be someone close in the family

Who'll alleviate some of your fear

We may want assistance for various things

We should not be ashamed to request

Asking someone for what we might need

Is easier than you might've guessed

Just the way you'd help if a friend came to you

They'd hope that you would do the same

So if ever you may need to, make a call

You'd surely be glad someone came

CHANGE THE WORLD

What can you do to change the world
And make it a better place?

What can you do to change this life
So God's children can embrace?

What can you do to stop bloodshed
And save the human race?

What can you do to change it soon
So that people cease to hate?

What can you do to stop the death
In the wars that they create?

You can spread the word of peace and love
And pray it's not too late

PERSEVERE

When one door is closing, don't hang your head

Another will open, use that instead

If you're facing a wall, just look around

There's always a different way to be found

It seems like a mountain blocking your will

But climb and discover it's just a small hill

So someone said 'no' and you feel life's a mess

You cannot give up, for you'll soon hear a 'yes'

You're scared of rejection, you must face that fear

For any successes, you must persevere

ONE LIFE

There was rain on my window
As I stared out into space
There were tears on my pillow
Which had dripped down from my face

There was pain in my chest
A thumping in my heart
And my brain couldn't rest
Was 'the end' about to start?

Then I was perspiring
My body soaking wet
Scared I was expiring
I wasn't ready yet

From feeling very anxious
I was in a world of black
It seems I fell unconscious …

But thank God I came back

I recall this episode
When for my life I fought
Travelling on that frightening road
Has changed the way I've thought

Being thankful that I'm still here
Has altered my old ways
My gratitude is so sincere
Now I won't waste my days

I don't fret now for what might be
I won't get quite so stressed
For healthy heart and mind for me
I'm sure that would be best

No complaining, that is my vow
Just so grateful on all fronts
For as far as we know right now
We will only live the once

PROMISES

He promised to stay faithful
While he worked away
It didn't take him very long
Before he chose to stray

She promised she'd stay sober
But secretly she drinks
She doesn't care that others talk
Or what anybody thinks

He promised he would visit
But words for him are cheap
Again he let his daughter down
She cried herself to sleep

She promised she would be there
To help her aging dad
She doesn't go, he sits and waits
For the girl that he once had

Never make a promise
If you think that you could break it
Rather than hurt loved ones
Better you don't make it

ANGEL

What is an angel?

Is it one of God's helpers who flies down here
  with wings?

Or are you one of those who ridicules such things?

Someone watching over you, is that what you
  believe?

Maybe that is too far-fetched for you to quite
  conceive

Relatives who have passed on, do they stay
  around to guide you?

Or is this just a longing that may linger deep inside
  you?

It can be a source of comfort when you might feel
  you're without it

That thought has helped so many that I wouldn't
  even doubt it

Could it be that angels are living in your street?

Ordinary people, the type we often meet

Good of soul and kind of heart - there's more than
  just a few

Could it be that an angel is there inside of you?

LAUGH

When things have gone wrong
Sometimes I've laughed
It wasn't that easy
And I know it sounds daft

But what's done is done
You made that mistake
It's probably an error
Anyone could make

Don't think you're stupid
Don't put yourself down
Don't be so sad now
Wipe off that frown

My life's not so serious
That I can't laugh at me
I don't have an ego
It's the best way to be

So just change your mind-set
From now for ever after
When you need to be lifted
You might just need some laughter

PARADISE

When there will be no fighting
And people stop inciting
Hatred against race of any kind

When there will be no killing
And people are not willing
To turn on other countries, we may find

That we can live without fear
And protect those who are dear
Wouldn't that all be very nice?

If racism just ends
We all could live as friends
And we would all be in Paradise

If there was no starvation
And no more deprivation
A wonderful world we could see

With no shortage of food
Good health would be renewed
To live better lives, we'd agree

If all had drinking water
And homes of bricks and mortar
There may be no more lives we sacrifice

If more children we could save
From a cold and silent grave
We could all then be in Paradise

If my true love could be you
I can say what I would do
I'd swear to stay forever and a day

If you say that we are one
And our story has begun
I will promise to love you in every way

So if you want me really
And you'll love me sincerely
You wouldn't need to ask me even twice

There is no one else before you
As I really do adore you
So I would truly be in Paradise

GETTING OLD

"I don't want to get old", I've heard them say

"When my hair and my skin and my outlook is grey"

"I don't want to get old", I've heard them wail

"When my hearing, my eyesight and my memory fail"

But as long as there are flowers with a wonderful smell

I'm surrounded by family with stories to tell

Friends to laugh with and enjoy the day

Children giggling while they learn and play

Puppies yapping, wanting some love

A beautiful night, a bright moon above

Excellent food, a cocktail or two

So much to see and so much to do

I want to get older because I want to live

I prefer to get older than the alternative

A BETTER YOU

You don't need to be the greatest in all you undertake

You don't have to be the icing on everybody's cake

You don't need to be the top dog in everything you do

Just always try to be a better you

You don't need to be the smartest of everyone you meet

You don't have to see all people as those you have to beat

You don't need to fly much higher than anybody flew

Just always try to be a better you

You don't need to push yourself so hard to always top the pile

You don't need to win and at such cost that you forget to smile

You don't need to show you're brighter than everyone you knew

Just always try to be a better you

You don't need to be superior to all those who may know you

You don't need to reach the highest peak so others stay below you

You don't need to win each argument with different points of view

Just always try to be a better you

REASONS

Do you ever ask what your purpose is?
Are you questioning why you are here?
Do you mean nothing in the scheme of things?
Does your reason for life seem unclear?

I will answer these questions
In the best way that I can
I'll start by saying that I believe
That we are all part of the plan

There are many reasons why we're here
Some I will try to explain
But firstly you must understand
We should give so much more than we gain

We are all here to do only good
And to teach and pass on what is right
To show love and caring to all God's people
To implore the whole world not to fight

We're here to help countries of the world
And make each one a better place
We must learn to 'love thy neighbour'
Whatever religion or race

We are all here to help those in need
The sick and the poor to begin with
Those on the streets or doing hard drugs
And all the lost souls they have been with

We are all here to help the infirm
And also the deaf and the blind
So we who are able need to assist
For it doesn't take much to be kind

Now these are just some of the answers I give
For more I could write through the seasons
But be assured when you ask why you're here
There are more than enough worthy reasons

NOTHING

He has a great big mansion
With lots of empty spaces
Grand designs grace every room
But they're void of any faces
So what he has means nothing

A country cottage too
But he holidays alone
He may have all mod cons
But no one calls his phone
So what he has means nothing

He has a private aeroplane
Which counts for diddly-squat
For he travels by himself
Despite the wealth he's got
So what he has means nothing

He likes to talk of what he owns
But somehow he can't seem to see
That I don't care about those things
They really mean nothing to me

CONTENTMENT

The feeling of contentment is so often underrated

But the importance of this mind state can't be
exaggerated

Striving for sheer happiness which can't just be created

Will mean you missing out on much and that can't be
overstated

The feeling of contentment is a warmth you feel inside

A certain look upon your face, a smile you cannot hide

Being thankful for what you have and joyful tears
you've cried

It's a mix of love and gratitude that keeps you satisfied

Remembering with fondness all the friends with good
intent

Laughing at those memories of the great times that
were spent

The many things that you've done with the love you
shared and meant

Add this all up to understand the meaning of content

TRUST YOURSELF

You must learn to trust yourself

To do what you think is right

In the brightness of the dawn

Or the stillness of the night

You must learn to trust yourself

To do what you think is best

At the sunrise from the east

To the sunset in the west

You must learn to trust yourself

To do what you think is just

With any choice that you make

You owe yourself that trust

You must learn to trust yourself

And know deep down inside

That the feeling in your gut

Is nature's greatest guide

GIVE A LITTLE

People are living on the streets
Sleeping under the sky
An awful world where no one eats
We can't just walk on by

Begging for coins to buy some food
While on the ground they lie
A cup of tea might lift their mood
We can at least but try

In freezing snow or thunderstorm
It cannot be denied
They haven't much to keep them warm
There's nowhere much to hide

There's a waiting list for a bed
When they can sleep inside
A safer place to rest their head
Before their soul has died

Real people who are sleeping rough
Both young and old it's true
Living a life that's very tough
With hopes to start anew

So give a little, help them climb
And realise when you do
At another place and different time
One of them could be you

TEACH THE CHILDREN

What kind of man do you want to be?

A pillar of society?

Walking tall with your head held high

To be held in such great esteem?

And Madam what would you like to do?

Earn the respect that may be due?

Straightened back as you're feeling proud

Would that be a part of your dream?

But what of your children, what will you teach?

Are you sure to practice that what you preach?

They are the future, show them well

That's important to the extreme

Tell them to love those from all nations

All faiths must have good relations

Compassion is the name of the game

Humanity's the name of the team

HAPPY TO BE HERE

I'm so very fortunate
In oh so many ways
I'll be saying 'Thank you'
For the rest of my days

I might not be here at all
As health was not my friend
But it was not my time to go
It worked out in the end

The experience did alter me
Now I'm more reflective
Without a shadow of a doubt
It changed my whole perspective

Now maybe more than ever
I'm happy with who I see
When I look in the mirror
At who's smiling back at me

I'm positive, I'm confident
I'm happy with my lot
I'm thankful, oh so grateful
For everything I've got

One thing I would not have known
If I hadn't made it through
Was the love for which I yearned
The love I have with you

YOUR TIME

You have often put others first

As choices go, that's not the worst

But when all is said and done

At times you must be number one

Though guilt might make you hesitate

I would suggest that you don't wait

To do what you need – that's not a crime

Take my advice as now is your time

It is not being selfish, you know it's true

For you can't help others if you don't help you

Look after yourself so you might stay well

And you will be happier as time will tell

So have a rest, yes take a good break

Not relaxing would be a mistake

Watch your health while you're still in your prime

Take my advice as now is your time

PLENTY

I hope you will see
How good life can be
If you understood just a fraction
That how much you've got
Is not worth a jot
And can't give you real satisfaction

If you'd comprehend
It's not what you spend
On things that you wouldn't use really
You've shoes by the score
And handbags galore
Some clothes you've not worn yet quite clearly

What matters is love
Not that other stuff
So give your life meaning with kindness
Let's not be greedy
Give to the needy
Put our selfish world right behind us

I hope for your sake
That it doesn't take
Until you're a hundred and twenty
For you to get wise
And then realise
That enough is actually plenty

WHAT IF

What if she didn't drink
So much alcohol?
What if she could've stayed
Away from it all?

What if he didn't get
Involved with cocaine?
What if he realised how
It damages his brain?

What if she didn't get
So mixed up with that crowd?
What if she had grown up
To make her family proud?

What if he didn't get
So angry with this life?
What if he'd chosen not
To carry that big knife?

What if they could say 'no'?
And what if they then found
That It might not be too late
To turn their lives around?

SLOW DOWN

It's your life, it's not a race

So just keep a steady pace

You'll enjoy what you see along the way

Take in all the scenery

Flowers and the greenery

Then you can appreciate every day

You may be a go-getter

But sometimes slow is better

At a hundred miles an hour you won't last

So if you drop your speed

You might find that indeed

You'll work smarter when you're going not too fast

Reduce stress by some measure

While you increase your pleasure

You must take back control before you drown

For your health and well-being

And to love what you're seeing

It's important that you really do slow down

BLESSINGS

I don't ask for jewels

Though there's beauty to behold

I don't want for very much

If the truth be told

Friends are my riches

Family is my gold

Love is my diamond

My blessings manifold

LOOKING BACK

Please say you danced all night
And your life was then enhanced
Say you swayed till morning light
Look back and say you danced

Please say you sang aloud
Those songs when you were young
Out singing with the crowd
Look back and say you've sung

Your smile was broad - I do hope so
As an adult and a child
For that's infectious, don't you just know
Look back and say you smiled

And say you laughed joyful tears
At the funny and the daft
Lots of giggles across the years
Look back and say you laughed

Say you loved in many ways
I hope that's what you'll tell
When you look back through all your days
Please say that you loved well

THE TRYING GAME

Here's a game that you could play

Leave out 'try' from what you say

If you manage and you might

Then leave it out from what you write

You can then replace the word

With others that you would have heard

Use 'intend' or maybe 'aim'

Either should still mean the same

But more confident you will sound

And you'll impress all those around

"I intend to win" – your strength will show

Rather than mean "I'll have a go"

You can also choose not to replace

Don't put a new word in the space

So "I will try to pass the test"

Becomes "I will pass" and be the best

Then when you've heard or when you've read

The words you've written or you've said

You'll have the belief that you need

And a better chance that you'll succeed

GIVING THANKS

Thank you for awakening me for each and every day

Thank you for enlightening me to see a better way

Thank you for the happiness when I am in need

Thank you for the guidance which helps me to succeed

Thank you for the life I live, and for keeping me so well

Thank you for the love you give, and the lessons that
you tell

Thank you for all that I have - a gift that never ends

Thank you for my family and for caring for my friends

Thank you for the sunny days and also for the rain

Thank you for the answered prayers for those who
suffer pain

Thank you for the comfort that loving you provides

Thank you for all these things and a whole lot more
besides

THE MESSENGER

The messenger rode into town on a stallion tall and white
As people gathered round he asked "Please could I stay
the night?"
He was helped down from the horse and then was kindly led
To a humble place nearby where he could rest his head

When dawn cracked with warming sun, the messenger
awoke
Then he emerged and people came, before the stranger
spoke
"I have come to teach you all the right way you should live
I have come to tell you it is love we all should give."

The townsfolk came in numbers great and sat down on
the ground
Waiting now to hear these words they hardly made a sound
The messenger began to speak in a most impassioned way
And as he walked among them all this is what they heard
him say

"You must love yourself enough so that others may love you
Love your friends and family and love your neighbours too
And you should give so much more than you care to receive
For these are the laws of love that you should all believe."

"No good can come from prejudice - no good can come
	from war
Work at peace throughout your lands and love each other
	more
Learn that white and black and brown is only outer skin
We are all cousins in this world, with blood of red within."

"Do show kindness and compassion wherever you may be
You should always give as you can - show generosity
Motivate and encourage - give others your support
These are all important things that you must now be
	taught."

"Always show your gratitude for everything that's good
And always do what is right, then all the people would
I only ask one more thing - please teach what you have
	heard
So I can be on my way for I must spread the word."